CONNECTICUT PATRIOTS

Their Lives, Contributions,
and Burial Sites

JOE FARRELL • LAWRENCE KNORR • JOE FARLEY

SUNBURY
PRESS

Mechanicsburg, PA USA

Published by Sunbury Press, Inc.
Mechanicsburg, Pennsylvania

SUNBURY
P R E S S
www.sunburypress.com

FIRST SUNBURY PRESS EDITION: April 2025

Set in Adobe Garamond | Interior design by Crystal Devine | Cover by Lawrence Knorr | Edited by the authors.

Publisher's Cataloging-in-Publication Data
Names: Farrell, Joe, author | Farley, Joe, author | Knorr, Lawrence, author.
Title: Connecticut patriots : their lives, contributions, and burial sites / Joe Farrell Lawrence Knorr Joe Farley.
Description: First trade paperback edition. | Mechanicsburg, PA : Sunbury Press, 2025.
Summary: The individuals from Connecticut who played prominent roles in the founding of the USA are detailed.
Identifiers: ISBN 979-8-88819-348-8 (softcover).
Subjects: HISTORY / United States / Revolutionary Period (1775-1800) | BIOGRAPHY & AUTOBIOGRAPHY / Political.

Designed in the USA
0 1 1 2 3 5 8 13 21 34 55

For the Love of Books!

Contents

Contents

Introduction

Probably the most famous Patriot from Connecticut was Noah Webster; he of dictionary fame. While his later contributions in lexicography defined the English language in an American context, few know he was an ardent Patriot as a thought leader, influencing the path of the Constitution as it was conceived and ratified.

Some would say we would not have a country without Connecticut lawyer Roger Sherman, who, with James Wilson, conceived of the Three-Fifths Compromise that kept South and North from separating at our founding. As seen from the Twenty-First Century, this agreement seems almost evil, yet it was the path forward to eventual freedom for all. Sherman is also the answer to a trivia question: Who is the only signer of all four of our founding documents?

But we do not lead off with either of these men. Rather Samuel Huntington claims the top spot as a Governor of Connecticut and the first President of the Confederation Congress, following the ratification of the Articles of Confederation, our first constitution, which defined the office more formally. Those who were Presidents of the Continental Congress before the Articles served in a traditional role with no formal guidelines. While lacking all the authority of the future role of President of the United States post-Constitution, this was a leadership role at a time before the victory at Yorktown and the Treaty of Paris.

Of course, great heroes were made in Connecticut. The young spy, Nathan Hale, regretted he had "but one life to give for his country." Old Israel Putnam urged the Patriots atop Breed's Hill to hold their fire "until they saw the whites of their eyes." Ethan Allen and Joseph Plumb Martin were both of Connecticut stock, though they ended up in other states, Allen in Vermont and Martin in Maine.

Major General Oliver Wolcott is probably one of the least lauded of the Patriots from Connecticut who deserves much more recognition. He was also the organizer of the melting of the statue of King George III into lead bullets.

William Samuel Johnson was reluctant to join the cause at first but became one of the most influential debaters during the Constitutional Convention and may have been the best-educated Founder.

Let us not overlook the surprising Andrew Adams, not related to John or Sam; Eliphalet Dyer, who had one of the most interesting names; Titus Hosmer, the great lawyer; and William Williams and his pure heart.

Please enjoy the retelling of our founding through the brief biographies of these citizens of Connecticut. Always remember: "Poor is the nation that has no heroes, but poorer still is the nation that having heroes, fails to remember and honor them." (attributed to Marcus Tullius Cicero)

Lawrence Knorr, Ph.D.
April 2025

Samuel Huntington
(1731–1796)

First President of the United States?

Buried at Colonial Cemetery (aka Old Norwichtown Cemetery),
Norwich, Connecticut.

———•———

**Continental Congress • Articles of Confederation
Declaration of Independence**

This founder happened to be the President of Congress on March 1, 1781, when the Articles of Confederation officially went into effect. The Articles essentially brought the individual colonies together and created the United States of America. It is because of his position in the Congress at the time that some point to this founder as the first president. Whether one agrees with that view is not important. The man can and should be remembered for his efforts on behalf and his contributions to the young country. Known for his great dignity and exceptional gentleness, he was described by those who knew him as "a sensible, candid and worthy man." He was among those who risked all by affixing his signature to the Declaration of Independence. His name was Samuel Huntington.

———◆———

Huntington was born on July 16, 1731, in what is now Scotland, Connecticut. He was the firstborn of Nathaniel and Mehetabel Huntington's ten children. Since he was the oldest of ten children, he was expected to work the family farm. As a result, according to multiple sources, he never received any formal education. However, one researcher has written that Huntington graduated from Yale College in 1755. Considering his later success, this is entirely possible. When he reached

Samuel Huntington

the age of 16, he apprenticed with a barrel maker while at the same time continuing to assist his father with the farm. He somehow found the time to educate himself by borrowing books from local attorneys and his future father in law, the Reverend Ebenezer Devotion. It appears possible that the studies he undertook on his own could have prepared him for Yale. What is not in dispute is fueled by his industry; he became a practicing attorney after being admitted to the Connecticut bar in 1754.

In 1761 Huntington married Martha Devotion, the daughter of the aforementioned Ebenezer. The couple did not have any children of their own, but when one of Huntington's brothers died, they adopted his two children. Huntington and his wife stayed together until she died in 1794. The couple's adopted son, Samuel Huntington, became the third governor of Ohio.

By the age of thirty, Huntington was one of the most important lawyers in Connecticut. In 1765 he was named the King's Attorney for the colony apposition, making him Connecticut's attorney general. When Huntington first entered politics a year before being appointed as the King's Attorney, as a member of the Connecticut General Assembly, he held conservative views and was loyal to the king. However, as the British Parliament began imposing oppressive measures on the colonies, his position changed, and he became an outspoken critic of the crown and resigned his office. In 1775 he was chosen along with Roger Sherman and Oliver Walcott to represent Connecticut in the Continental Congress. All three members of the Connecticut delegation were ardent advocates of independence. As a member of Congress, he voted for American independence and signed the declaration that proclaimed the separation of the colonies from the British empire.

In terms of his congressional service, in 1846 the historian Robert T. Conrad wrote that Huntington "devoted his talents and time to the public service. His stern integrity, and inflexible patriotism, rendered him a prominent member, and attracted a large share of the current business of the house; as a member of numerous important committees, he acted with judgment and deliberation, and cheerfully and perseveringly dedicated his moments of leisure to the general benefit of the country."

Huntington was not known as a great orator, nor did he write much or very well. He earned the respect of his fellow delegates through his diligence and hard work. When John Jay left Congress to become minister to Spain, Huntington was elected to succeed him as president in 1779. On March 1, 1781, the Articles of Confederation were signed, which made the thirteen colonies the United States of America. Because Huntington was the President of Congress, some point to him as the first President of the United States.

Five months after the signing of the Articles, Huntington was forced to resign from Congress and return to Connecticut due to illness. Despite battling health issues for the rest of his days, he remained active in public affairs. He served as chief justice of the Connecticut Supreme Court and as lieutenant governor of the state before serving as the third governor of the Constitution State. He advocated for religious tolerance, the abolition of slavery, and the ratification of the United States Constitution under which George Washington served as the generally recognized first president of the country. Huntington presided over the state convention that gathered to debate ratification.

In 1900 Susan Huntington wrote about her ancestor in the *Connecticut Magazine*:

> Among the phalanx of Patriots who fearlessly and unbrokenly re-sisted the menaces and efforts of the British government to prevent the Declaration of Independence, it is remarkable to observe the great proportion that arouse from the humble walks of life who by the vigour [*sic*] of their intellect, and unwearied fearlessness com-pensated the deficiencies of early education and enrolled them-selves with honor and capacity among the champions of Colonial freedom. Such a man was Samuel Huntington . . . His extreme modesty and the fact that he left no descendants perhaps account for so little appreciation of the value of his services in these days of revival of interest in all things relating to the American Revolution.

Tomb of Samuel Huntington

Huntington was serving as governor when he died on January 5, 1796. He was laid to rest just 15 miles away from the place of his birth in the Old Norwichtown Cemetery that is now known as the Colonial Cemetery. In 2003 the citizens of Norwich raised $31,000 and used the funds to exhume both Huntington and his wife. The tomb was restored, and the bodies of the founder and his wife were placed in new caskets and reinterred. There rests a man who went from being a barrel maker to a signer of the Declaration of Independence, to become, at least according to the people of Norwich, the first President of the United States.

Andrew Adams
(1736–1797)

Connecticut's Chief Justice

Buried at West Cemetery
Litchfield, Connecticut

———•—•———

**Continental Congress • Articles of Confederation
Militiaman**

Perhaps the least famous of the Founders named Adams, Andrew was
a Continental Congressman from Connecticut who signed the Articles
of Confederation. He was also a colonel in the Connecticut Militia
and rose to be the Chief Justice of the Supreme Court in Connecticut.
Unfortunately, no known portrait survives.

———•◦•———

Andrew Adams, the son of Samuel Adams (1703-1788) and his
wife, Mary (née Fairchild) Adams (1698-1803), was born in Stratford,
Connecticut, on January 7, 1736. No, this was not the famous Samuel
Adams of Boston, who was active in the Sons of Liberty. This Samuel
Adams was a lawyer from Connecticut who was no relation to the Boston
Adamses. In addition to practicing law, this Samuel Adams was a judge
in Fairfield County.

Young Andrew first received the traditional "classical education" in
local schools and then followed in his father's footsteps into the law, attending Yale, where he graduated in 1760. He then studied law under
his father and first practiced with him in Stamford. By 1764, Adams
opened his practice in Litchfield, Connecticut, and soon became one of
the leading attorneys there.

York Courthouse where the Articles of Confederation were approved

Adams married Eunice Buel, the youngest daughter of Judge Samuel and Abigail (Peck) Canfield of New Milford, Connecticut. The couple had one child, a son named Andrew.

In 1772, Adams was named the king's attorney for the County of Litchfield. He and his family moved there in 1774, where he spent the rest of his life. Adams was also a Freemason in Litchfield as a member of St. Paul's Lodge No. 11.

Adams became involved in politics and was elected to several minor positions in the Litchfield area. As the tensions began to rise between the colonies and Great Britain, Adams was appointed to the Connecticut Council of Safety for two years. When hostilities broke out at Lexington and Concord, Adams volunteered for the Connecticut militia and rose to the rank of colonel during his service. In 1776, Adams was elected to the Connecticut House of Representatives, serving until 1781. He was the speaker in 1779 and 1780.

On October 11, 1777, Adams was elected to the Second Continental Congress, then meeting in York, Pennsylvania, and negotiating the Articles of Confederation. Adams was unable to attend that year, instead joining in 1778 when the Congress returned to Philadelphia. There, on July 9, 1778, at Independence Hall, Adams was one of the first to sign the Articles of Confederation as a delegate from Connecticut. During his remaining time in Congress, Adams was consulted about military affairs in New England and was proactive in seeking funding.

When Adams returned to Connecticut the next year, Governor Trumbull named him to the Connecticut Executive Council and appointed him as a judge on the Connecticut Supreme Court. He also continued to serve in the Connecticut Militia until the end of the war.

In 1793, Adams rose to Chief Justice of the Connecticut Supreme Court. He also earned his LL.D. (Doctorate in Law) degree from Yale in 1796.

Andrew Adams died at the age of 61 in Litchfield, Connecticut, on November 26, 1797. He was interred at what was then called the "East Cemetery" in Litchfield but is now known as West Cemetery. As of 1909, historian Dwight C. Kilbourn had visited Adams' grave and noted it was "a rapidly crumbling marble slab." The stone read:

> In memory of the Hon. Andrew Adams, Esq., Chief Judge of the
> Superior Court, who died November 27, 1797, in the 63d year of

Grave of Andrew Adams

his age. Having filled many distinguished offices with great ability and dignity, he was promoted to the highest judicial office in the State, which he held for several years, in which his eminent talents shone with uncommon lustre, and were exerted to the great advantage of the public and the honor of the High Court in which he presided. He made an early profession of religion, and zealously sought to protect its true Interests. He lived a Life and died the Death of a Christian. His filial Piety and paternal tenderness are held in sweet Remembrance.

A new granite memorial has since been placed next to the decrepit memorial.

Ethan Allen
(1738–1789)

Leader of the Green Mountain Boys

Buried at Green Mountain Cemetery
Burlington, Vermont

━━━◆◆━━━

Ethan Allen is a Revolutionary War hero who was a general in the Continental Army best known as the founder of the famous Green Mountain Boys. He is also known for his tireless and controversial effort to make Vermont independent from Britain, other colonies, and perhaps even from the U.S.

━━━◆◆━━━

Allen was born in Litchfield, Connecticut, on January 21, 1738, the first born to Joseph and Mary Allen. The family moved to Cornwall, and the Allens had seven more children, five boys and two girls. He began studies under a minister in the nearby town of Salisbury and hoped to gain admission to Yale. That plan was changed when his father died in 1755. He volunteered for militia service during the French and Indian War but saw no action and returned to Cornwall. He met and married Mary Brownson after a short courtship and took part ownership with his brother Heman in an iron furnace in Salisbury. There he bought a small farm and kept developing his iron business. The marriage was an unhappy one. They had five children, two of whom survived to adulthood. Mary died in 1783.

During his time in Salisbury, Allen met Thomas Young, a doctor. They had common interests in philosophy and political theory and decided to collaborate on a book. Young had convinced Allen to become a

Ethan Allen

Deist, i.e., the philosophical position that rejects revelation as a source of divine knowledge and asserts that reason and observation of the natural world are sufficient to determine the existence of god. The book was intended as an attack on organized religion. They worked on it until 1764, when Young moved away, taking the manuscript with him.

In the late 1760s, New Hampshire Governor Benning Wentworth sold land grants west of the Connecticut River. Allen bought grants for about 1000 acres. New York had issued land grants to much of the same land, and the dispute rose to the attention of the New York Supreme Court in 1770. New York won the suit, and Wentworth's grants were declared fraudulent. After the trial, Allen met with other grant holders at Catamount Tavern in Bennington. At this meeting, the settlers formed a militia group to defend their land. They called themselves The Green Mountain Boys and chose Allen as their leader. For the next four years, they fought against New York authorities to keep their land. The New

York legislature branded Allen and others as outlaws and offered a reward for their capture.

It was well known throughout New England that there were cannon and artillery at the British forts at Ticonderoga and Crown Point. Following the Battles of Lexington and Concord, a Connecticut militia asked Allen if he and his men would help them capture the forts. He agreed, and the Green Mountain Boys joined 60 men from Massachusetts and Connecticut in a meeting in Bennington on May 2. They planned a dawn raid for May 10. Not long after the Connecticut expedition was launched, the Massachusetts Committee of Safety launched its own expedition with Benedict Arnold in command. On the afternoon of May 9, they met, and Arnold asserted his right to command. The men refused to follow Arnold, and privately Allen and Arnold reached a deal that they would both lead the attack.

The British at Ticonderoga and Crown Point were not aware that war had broken out and were not expecting an attack of any kind. On May 10, 1775, Allen, Arnold, and the Green Mountain Boys stormed the fort at Ticonderoga and captured it with almost no resistance.

The victorious Americans quickly made plans for a strike against Crown Point. Led by Captain Seth Warner, a detachment of the Green Mountain Boys captured the small garrison there. The capture of Fort Ticonderoga and Crown Point proved to be important in the Revolutionary War because it secured protection from the British to the north and provided vital cannon for the colonial army.

When the Continental Congress found out about the capture of the fort, there was concern that it may have ruined any chance at reconciliation with Britain. Congress asked Allen to take the cannon and artillery to the southern end of Lake George so that inventory could be taken. Allen refused the request and argued that removing the weapons from the fort would leave the fort defenseless and leave the colonists in the western territories vulnerable to attack. As long as the cannon and artillery remained at the fort, they could be used to control traffic on Lake Champlain.

The cannon and artillery from Ticonderoga were eventually retrieved by Henry Knox and taken to Boston, where they were used to fortify Dorchester Heights and other areas around the city. Once Dorchester Heights was fortified, the British were forced to evacuate Boston.

On June 22, Allen and Seth Warner appeared before Congress in Philadelphia, where they argued for the inclusion of the Green Mountain Boys in the Continental Army. Congress agreed to establish a regiment of the Green Mountain Boys and agreed to pay them army rates for their service at Ticonderoga. When the regiment met, they held a vote to determine command. Seth Warner was elected to lead the regiment. He was viewed as a more stable and quieter choice than Allen.

Allen took the rejection in stride and wasted no time in joining Brigadier General Richard Montgomery's invasion of Canada. Operating an independent command ahead of the main body, he botched an attack on Montreal and was captured on September 25. He spent the next two and a half years as a British prisoner, enduring harsh conditions in British castles, New York City jails, and on prison ships. Allen was the type of Yankee the British loved to hate. He was a natural-born leader, brilliant, fearless, crude, bullheaded, arrogant, impulsive, egotistical, confrontational, physically imposing, and principled. General Prescott, the military governor of Montreal, put Allen in irons for 30 days and, with great fanfare, sent him to London to be executed. He arrived at Falmouth, England, after crossing under filthy conditions and was imprisoned in Pendennis Castle, Cornwall. In the meantime, Prescott was captured trying to escape Montreal. King George, fearing for Prescott's fate, decreed that American prisoners should be sent back to America and treated as prisoners of war.

Meanwhile, in January 1777, Vermont declared its independence from Great Britain and land claims from New York and New Hampshire to become the Republic of Vermont, which existed for fourteen years. Though an ally to the American colonies, the Continental Congress did not recognize them, referring to them as "The New Hampshire Grants." Remarkably, slavery was outlawed in the republic.

In August 1777, Allen, while in custody in New York, learned of the death of his young son Joseph due to smallpox. In May 1778, he was exchanged for Colonel Archibald Campbell and reported to George Washington at Valley Forge. He would see no further action in the war.

Allen spent the next several years involved in Vermont's political and military matters and served as commander of the state's militia with the rank of Major General. During this time, some in Vermont negoitated a unification with Quebec, which was agreeable to the British, but following the surrender at Yorktown, Vermont sided with the Americans.

Statue of Ethan Allen at Fort Ticonderoga

On February 16, 1784, Allen married Frances "Fanny" Montresor Brush Buchanan after a brief courtship, and they had three children. That same year, Allen recovered the Deist manuscript from the estate of Thomas Young and had it published as *Reason: The Only Oracle of Man*. It is considered the first work published in the United States that openly attacked Christianity. The book was a financial and critical failure and undermined Allen's reputation as an iconic American Patriot.

On February 12, 1789, Allen died at his home in Burlington after suffering an apoplectic fit. He was buried in Green Mountain Cemetery in Burlington. The exact location of his remains within the cemetery is unknown. The magnificent columnar monument marking his grave may or may not actually be over his remains. Attempts have been made to settle the issue, including subsurface radar scans to detect remains, but the scans have remained inconclusive. The uncertainty has fueled an ongoing local controversy over the true burial site.

Vermont finally achieved statehood in 1791, after Allen's death.

Grave of Ethan Allen

Eliphalet Dyer
(1721–1807)

"... an honest, worthy man ..."

Buried at Windham Cemetery
Windham, Connecticut

———

**Continental Congress • Continental Association
Militiaman**

Eliphalet Dyer had one of the more unusual names among Continental Congressmen. "Eliphalet" was derived from Hebrew, meaning "God who delivers." Congressman Dyer certainly "delivered" for his constituents in Windham, Connecticut, throughout a long political career. Dyer was variously a lawyer, jurist, and statesman who was a delegate to the Continental Congress and signed the Continental Association.

———

Dyer was born in Windham, Connecticut, on September 14, 1721, the son of Thomas Dyer and his wife, Lydia (née Backus) Dyer. The elder Dyer was a native of Weymouth, Massachusetts, who moved to Connecticut circa 1715. There, he married Lydia, the daughter of John Backus of Windham. Upon settling in Windham, Thomas served in the Connecticut General Assembly and rose to become a major in the Windham County militia.

Young Eliphalet was taught "preparatory studies" prior to enrolling at Yale College (now Yale University) in New Haven in 1740. Dyer was already a town clerk as a teenager and studied law at Yale. In May 1745, he married Huldah Bowen of Providence, Rhode Island, the daughter of

ELIPHALET DYER
Member of the Continental Congress

Eliphalet Dyer

Colonel Jacob Bowen. Upon graduating from Yale, Dyer was admitted to the colonial bar in 1746 and practiced law in Windham.

Following in his father's footsteps, Dyer joined the militia and was elected justice of the peace and to the colonial assembly in 1747. He served in sessions in that body in 1747, 1748, 1753, and 1753, and then from 1756 to 1784. During this time, he became directly embroiled in territorial disputes between Connecticut and Pennsylvania. In 1754, the Susquehanna Land Company published in Philadelphia a claim that

Connecticut's grant included the lands westward as "far as the South Sea." This happened to carve off the northern tier of William Penn's colony. The Connecticut General Assembly was lobbied to permit Connecticut's citizens to settle the lands, but the outbreak of the French and Indian War distracted from this.

During the war, Dyer was a lieutenant colonel in the Connecticut militia, participating in the capture of Crown Point in 1755. He was promoted to lieutenant and led a regiment in the 1758 attack on Canada.

After the war, in 1763, Dyer traveled to London representing the Susquehanna River land claim but was turned down due to the just-passed Proclamation Line Act, which established set boundaries for the colonies. Unfortunately, this was unsatisfactory for many Connecticut settlers who had invested in land, leading to conflicts known as the Yankee-Pennamite Wars. Three times, hostilities flared between Pennsylvania and Connecticut. Ultimately, after the Revolution, the region was affixed to Pennsylvania by the Continental Congress, and Pennsylvania permitted the Yankees to stay as Pennsylvania citizens.

In September 1765, Dyer was a representative from Connecticut in the Stamp Act Congress. He was then elected a justice on the superior court in 1766, holding the post until 1793. He was chief justice after 1789.

As the American Revolution began to simmer, Dyer was named to Connecticut's Committee of Safety. In July 1774, when the Committee of Correspondence met regarding a delegate to the First Continental Congress, Dyer was selected to represent the colony in Philadelphia. He served in Congress until 1775, then 1777 to 1779, and finally from 1782 to 1783.

On October 20, 1774, Dyer signed the Continental Association, banning certain British imports, including tea. Dyer was not in Congress when it moved to York following the invasion of Philadelphia, but he did return to Philadelphia to hear the final debates about the Articles of Confederation although he was not a signer. In his diary, John Adams described Dyer as "longwinded and roundabout, obscure and cloudy, very talkative and very tedious, yet an honest, worthy man; means and judges well."

After leaving Congress, Yale conferred a Doctor of Divinity degree to Dyer in 1787. He continued to serve as a judge in Connecticut, retiring in 1793 as the chief justice. Dyer died on May 13, 1807, at age 85, and was buried at Windham Cemetery.

The Litchfield Monitor of Connecticut stated, "Died, at Windham, the Hon. ELIPHALET DYER, in the 87th year of his age. He was distinguished for his useful talents and the faithful and honourable discharge of his important duties."

Grave of Eliphalet Dyer

New York's *The Morning Chronicle* said, "He was one of those illustrious patriots (whose name will live in the annals of our nation to all posterity) who signed and assisted in supporting the Declaration of Independence in 1776, which was the keystone to the 'wide arch of our rais'd empire.'"

Well, contrary to the New York paper declaring so, Dyer never signed the Declaration of Independence and was not in Congress at the time to debate or pass the measure. As Mark Twain once said, "If you don't read the newspaper, you're uninformed. If you read the newspaper, you're misinformed."

Fortunately, you have our series of books to sort out a most accurate account of the accomplishments and contributions of our Founders.

Nathan Hale
(1755–1776)

"But One Life"

Buried at Nathan Hale Cemetery (cenotaph)
South Coventry, Connecticut

Hero and Martyr

Nathan Hale was a young Connecticut Patriot who spied for the Continental Army and was captured and executed by the British. Ever since he has been lauded as a hero for his devotion to the Patriot cause despite his young age.

Hale, born June 6, 1755, in Coventry, Connecticut, was the son of Deacon Richard Hale, a minister, and his wife, Elizabeth (née Strong) Hale. The elder Hale was a descendant of the Reverend John Hale of the Salem witch trials of 1692.

From 1769 to 1773, Hale attended Yale College with his older brother Enoch. While there, they befriended fellow student Benjamin Tallmadge, who later became a spy for the Patriot cause. The Hale brothers were members of the Linonian Society of Yale, a debate club that discussed the issues and culture of the day. Hall graduated with honors at age 18 and became a teacher in East Haddam and then New London.

Following the Battles of Lexington and Concord, Hale joined the Connecticut Militia. Possibly concerned about his teaching contract that was set to expire in July 1775, Hale stayed behind when his company was involved in the Siege of Boston. On July 4, 1775, Hale received a letter

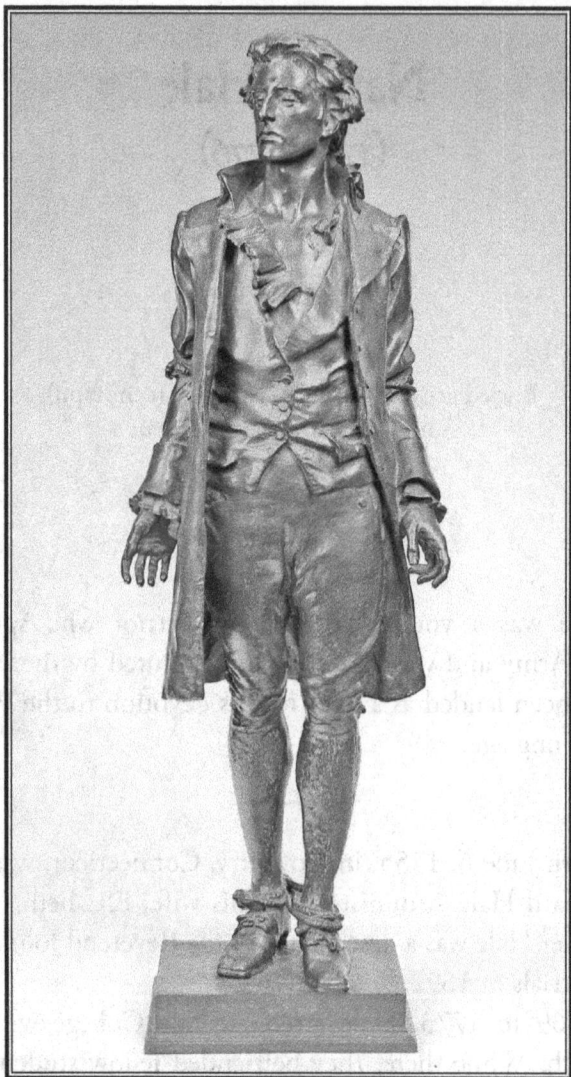

Bronze statue of Nathan Hale

from his friend Benjamin Tallmadge, who was in Boston to witness the siege. Wrote Tallmadge:

> Was I in your condition, I think the more extensive service would be my choice. Our holy Religion, the honor of our God, a glorious country, & a happy constitution is what we have to defend.

Hale was so inspired by the letter that he rejoined the 7th Connecticut Regiment led by Colonel Charles Webb and was commissioned as a first lieutenant. As the Siege of Boston ended and the focus shifted to New York City, Hale joined Knowlton's Rangers, the first organized intelligence unit in the Continental Army. Lieutenant Colonel Charles Knowlton and his men helped to defend Manhattan. As the British routed the Continentals on Long Island, General Washington escaped from Brooklyn Heights to Manhattan under cover of darkness. When the commander in chief, via Knowlton, called for a spy to serve behind enemy lines on Long Island, Hale was the only volunteer, the others preferring to risk dying in battle rather than in disguise. Thus, Hale, disguised as a Dutch schoolteacher seeking work, was ferried across the Long Island Sound to Huntington, New York, on September 12, 1776.

Unfortunately, on September 15, the British invaded the southern tip of Manhattan, forcing Washington to Harlem Heights on the north end of the island. On September 21, the Great New York Fire of 1776 blazed through the town. Some thought the Americans sabotaged the city, but Washington and the Congress had rejected the idea. The Americans accused the British of burning and sacking the town. Regardless, after the fire, more than 200 Patriots were detained for questioning, Hale being one of them.

There are conflicting accounts as to how Hale was caught. Consider Tiffany, a Loyalist Connecticut shopkeeper, related that Major Robert Rogers of the Queen's Rangers recognized Hale at a tavern and duped him by pretending to be a Patriot. He then took him into custody in Queens, near Flushing Bay. Another possibility involved a Loyalist cousin, Samuel Hale, who betrayed him.

Regardless, Hale was searched and interrogated. It is said General William Howe questioned him himself. That night, Hale was either held in a greenhouse or one of the bedrooms of Howe's headquarters. His requests for a Bible and clergyman were both denied. He was permitted to write two letters, one to his brother Enoch and the other to his commanding officer. Both were never sent. They were torn up the next morning in front of Hale.

That morning, September 22, 1776, Nathan Hale was marched along the Post Road to the Park of Artillery next to the Dove Tavern

EXECUTION OF CAPTAIN HALE.

Execution of Captain Hale

(currently 66th Street and 3rd Ave in Manhattan). There, he was hanged by the British as a spy. He was only 21 years old. All accounts state Hale composed himself very well despite the situation. Wrote British officer Frederick McKensie, who was present:

> He behaved with great composure and resolution, saying he thought it the duty of every good Officer, to obey any orders given him by his Commander-in-Chief; and desired the Spectators to be at all times prepared to meet death in whatever shape it might appear.

There were no official records of Hale's final words. According to tradition, based on the account of British Captain John Montresor, a witness, he famously said, "I only regret that I have but one life to lose for my country." Montresor had spoken to American Captain William Hull the next day under a flag of truce. Hull recorded in his memoirs the following related by Montresor:

"On the morning of his execution," continued the officer, "my station was near the fatal spot, and I requested the Provost Marshal [William Cunningham] to permit the prisoner to sit in my marquee, while he was making the necessary preparations. Captain Hale entered: he was calm, and bore himself with gentle dignity, in the consciousness of rectitude and high intentions. He asked for writing materials, which I furnished him: he wrote two letters, one to his mother and one to a brother officer. He was shortly after summoned to the gallows. But a few persons were around him, yet his characteristic dying words were remembered. He said, 'I only regret, that I have but one life to lose for my country.'"

Some scholars believe Hale was paraphrasing or quoting lines from a popular play, *Cato*, which he was likely familiar with:

How beautiful is death, when earn'd by virtue!
Who would not be that youth? What pity is it
That we can die but once to serve our country.

There are varying accounts of what he said or how it was said. Most likely, the British officer was only telling the most prominent line of a much longer speech. Regardless, it was certainly a tragic and profound moment.

Besides the 66th Street and 3rd Avenue location, City Hall Park and Grand Central Terminal both claim to be the hanging site. A plaque hung by the Daughters of the American Revolution at the Yale Club at 44th Street and Vanderbilt Avenue claims the event occurred near the club. Grand Central Terminal is only feet away.

Hale's body was not recovered by the family and has been lost to time. They erected a memorial with an empty grave at the Nathan Hale Cemetery in South Coventry, Connecticut.

Nathan Hale is one of the most memorialized of all Patriots. He has had numerous statues and portraits made, though there are no known paintings of him in life. His name has been assigned to buildings, schools, forts, ships, and towns. He has appeared on several postage stamps. His ancestral home is also a historic site, and there are numerous markers throughout Long Island and Manhattan.

A full-sized statue of Hale was unveiled in Langley, Virginia, at CIA headquarters on June 6, 1973, the bicentennial of his graduation from Yale. In a statement at that time, Hale was said to be "the country's first intelligence officer." According to Agency tradition, an officer who places a Washington quarter at Hale's statue when leaving on an assignment will return safely.

Monument to Nathan Hale

Titus Hosmer
(1736–1780)

Connecticut Lawyer

Buried at Mortimer Cemetery,
Middletown, Connecticut.

———◆·◆———

Articles of Confederation

Titus Hosmer was a lawyer and leading politician from Connecticut who
was thrice elected to the Continental Congress but only attended briefly
for one of his terms. He signed the Articles of Confederation.

———◆·◆———

Titus Hosmer was born in West Hartford, Connecticut, in either 1736 or 1737, the son of Captain Stephen Hosmer and his wife,
Deliverance (née Graves) Hosmer. Titus was the third son among eight
children. The Hosmer family originated in Kent, England. An ancestor
emigrated to Newtown, Massachusetts, in the early 1600s.

Young Titus was educated in local schools as a youth. He then attended Yale College in New Haven. In a speech in 1850, scholar David
Dudley said of Hosmer, "While at Yale College, he was distinguished for
the acquisition of sciences, excelled in the languages and fine writing.
Being graduated in 1757, [he] settled in Middletown about 1760."

Shortly after graduation, Hosmer was admitted to the Connecticut
colonial bar and began practicing law in Middletown. The following
year, he married Lydia Lord, and the two began a family. Throughout
the 1760s, Hosmer gradually increased in stature as a lawyer, working on
important estates and dealing with the disposition of debts and creditors.

Titus Hosmer

Meanwhile, seven children were born during these years, including Stephen Titus Hosmer, who would later become chief justice of the Connecticut Supreme Court, and Hezekiah Lord Hosmer, who became a U. S. representative for the state of New York.

As Hosmer became better known, he entered politics, first in local offices such as justice of the peace. Following the collapse of royal rule in Connecticut, Hosmer was elected to the Connecticut General Assembly in October 1773, holding this seat until 1778. A strong advocate for independence, Hosmer was elected speaker of the state House of Representatives in 1777. He also served as a member of the local Committee of Safety.

As an emerging leader in the Connecticut assembly, Hosmer was elected to the Continental Congress three times: first on November 3, 1774; next on October 12, 1775; and again, on October 11, 1777. However, he only attended in 1778, including when the Congress was in York, Pennsylvania. There is no record as to why he did not attend but a few months, but some have speculated he may have been in poor health. Another possibility is the size of his family and the need to be close to home. Yet another is his attention to duty in the Connecticut Assembly, where he was the speaker and then a state senator beginning in May 1778. Regardless, records show he did attend sessions from June 23 to September 10, 1778, when he returned home.

Hosmer could have been a signer of the Continental Association, and the Declaration of Independence had he been in Philadelphia to fulfill his elected duties. However, it seems he had competing duties and opted to lead locally until the opportunity arose to sign the first constitution for the nation, the Articles of Confederation. The document had been negotiated the preceding two years and was reviewed by Congress during Hosmer's tenure. Starting on July 9, 1778, in Philadelphia, the delegates began to sign the document, after which it went to the states for ratification. Hosmer was one of five Connecticut delegates to sign. The others included Roger Sherman, Samuel Huntington, Oliver Wolcott, and Andrew Adams.

According to two letters written to Connecticut governor Johnathan Trumbull following the signing of the Articles, there was not much to do in Congress. Hosmer complained of the lack of progress with settling the debts of the army. He suggested the idleness was depressing him, and he worried about the continuing disagreements with the Southern States, suggesting the union might not hold together. He also reported on the behavior of some in Congress. Wrote Hosmer,

> . . . When we are assembled, several gentlemen have such a knack at starting questions of order, raising debates upon critical, captious, and trifling amendments, protracting them by long speeches, by postponing, calling for the previous question, and other arts, that it is almost impossible to get an important question decided at one

Titus Hosmer's grave

sitting; and if it is put over to another day, the field is open to be gone over again, precious time is lost, and the public business left undone . . .

Upon returning to Connecticut, Hosmer continued as a state senator and was then elected as a judge on the maritime Court of Appeals in January 1780. Unfortunately, Hosmer was not able to take the seat. He died suddenly on August 4, 1780. Obituaries did not mention a cause of death despite his young age of only 43 or 44. He was laid to rest in Mortimer Cemetery in Middletown, Connecticut. Diplomat and poet Joel Barlow wrote a moving tribute to Hosmer entitled "An Elegy." Wrote Barlow:

> Come to my soul, O shade of Hosmer, come Tho' doubting senates ask thy aid in vain; Attend the drooping virtues round thy tomb, And hear a while the orphan'd Muse complain.

Lydia followed Titus to the grave in 1798 and is buried next to him. Besides the sons mentioned previously, a grandson, also named Hezekiah Lord Hosmer, was an accomplished author and the first Chief Justice of the Montana Territory.

William Samuel Johnson
(1727–1819)

The Great Conciliator

Buried at Christ Episcopal Church Cemetery,
Stratford, Connecticut.

———◆———

U.S. Constitution • Continental Congress • U.S. Senate

William Samuel Johnson was one of the best educated of the Founders and, like others, had strong ties with England, which made renouncing the king personally tricky. He lived in London for four years (1767–1771) and had many good friends in England. Torn by conflicting loyalties, he remained neutral during the Revolution, speaking out only against extremism on both sides. Once independence was achieved, Johnson felt free to participate in the government. He thus served in the Confederation Congress, representing Connecticut (1785–1787), and played a significant role as a delegate to the Constitutional Convention. He was one of thirty-nine signers of the Constitution who together represented twelve states. Later he represented Connecticut in the United States Senate and served as the third president of Kings College, now known as Columbia University.

———◆———

William Samuel Johnson was born in Stratford, Connecticut, on October 7, 1727. His father was a well-known Anglican clergyman and later president of Kings College. His mother was Charity Floyd Nicoll, who was born in Long Island and died in 1758. Johnson received his primary education at home. He then went to Yale and graduated in 1744.

William Samuel Johnson (1727–1819)

William Samuel Johnson

In 1747 he was awarded a master of arts degree from Yale, and an honorary master's from Harvard.

He was under considerable pressure from his father to become a minister but resisted and chose to study law and gained admission to the bar. He set up a practice in Stratford, representing clients from nearby New York as well as Connecticut. Before long, he had established business connections with various mercantile houses in New York City. In 1749 he married Anne Beach, a local businessman's daughter, and they had five daughters and six sons. Sadly, many of them died before reaching adulthood. In the 1750s, Johnson joined the Connecticut militia and earned the rank of colonel.

His political involvement began in the Connecticut legislature. He served in the lower house in 1761 and 1765 and the upper house in

1766 and 1771-1775. He also served on the colony's supreme court in the years 172-1774. In between his service in the legislature from 1767 to 1771, Johnson lived in London, serving as Connecticut's agent in its attempt to settle the colony's claim to Mohegan lands in eastern Connecticut. He won the case and made many friends in England during this time, and Oxford awarded him an honorary degree in 1766. He sharply criticized British policy toward the colonies while there. He had attended the Stamp Act Congress in 1765 and served on the committee that drafted an address to the king, arguing the right of the colonies to decide tax policies for themselves. He also had opposed the Townshend Acts passed by Parliament in 1767 to pay for the French and Indian War. Now his experience in England convinced him that the British policies were shaped more by ignorance of American conditions than through sinister designs of a wicked government as many Patriots alleged.

As the Patriots became more radical in their demands for independence, Johnson was skeptical and found it challenging to commit to it. He thought that an independent America would quickly factionalize and become the easy victim of foreign invaders who would become our new enemy. He decided to work for peace between England and the colonies and to oppose extremism on both sides. He was a very prudent and cautious man who abhorred open conflict and violence. His legal background and his religious practices led him to favor peaceful solutions to disputes. It was by quiet diplomacy that he had become part of Connecticut's political elite. He was so highly thought of he was elected to the First Continental Congress in 1774, but he refused to participate; a move strongly criticized by the Patriots who removed him from militia command. He was also strongly criticized when he visited with British commander General Thomas Gage to end hostilities after Lexington and Concord. That led to his arrest for communicating with the enemy, but the charges were eventually dropped.

Remarkably Johnson's pro-peace activities never seriously damaged his prestige. Once the war was over, he resumed his political career. He served in the Confederation Congress from 1785 to 1787, where it is said he was one of the most popular and influential delegates. He was selected to represent Connecticut as a delegate to the Constitutional

Convention in 1787, along with Oliver Ellsworth and Roger Sherman. There he played a significant role. His expressive and eloquent speeches around the topic of representation had great weight in the debate. He favored a strong federal government to protect the rights of Connecticut and other small states from encroachment by their larger neighbors. He supported the New Jersey Plan, which called for a unicameral legislature with equal representation of the states. Later he gave his full support to the Connecticut Compromise, which called for a bicameral legislature with the upper house (Senate) providing equal representation for all states.

Towards the end of the convention, the delegates appointed a committee to revise and arrange the articles agreed upon. Johnson was appointed chair of the committee. Other notable committee members were Alexander Hamilton, Gouverneur Morris, James Madison, and Rufus King. On September 17, 1787, 39 delegates representing 12 states signed the Constitution, including Johnson. Three delegates (Randolph, Mason, and Gerry) refused to sign, and Rhode Island refused to participate. Johnson went on to play an active role in Connecticut's ratification process, emphasizing the advantages that would accrue to the small states under the Constitution.

Johnson became the first president of Columbia College in 1787 and became one of Connecticut's first senators in 1789. Johnson played a significant role in shaping the Judiciary Act of 1789, a critical law that established the federal judiciary system's details. He generally supported Hamiltonian measures that sought to strengthen the role of the executive in the federal government. When the federal government moved from New York to Philadelphia at the end of the first congress in 1791, Johnson resigned to retain his position at Columbia, where he successfully recruited faculty and improved the school's reputation for scholarship.

Johnson retired from Columbia in 1800, a few years after his wife died, and married Mary Brewster Beach, a relative of his first wife. They lived at his birthplace in Stratford, where he died in 1819 at the age of 92. He is buried in Christ Episcopal Church Cemetery in Stratford, Connecticut.

A favorite expression of Johnson's that gives insight into his personality and success is "To keep your secret is wisdom; to expect others to keep it is folly."

William Samuel Johnson's grave

Joseph Plumb Martin
(1760 – 1850)

Private Yankee Doodle

Buried at Sandy Point Cemetery.
Stockton Springs, Maine.

Military

Joseph Plumb Martin was a Connecticut militiaman and member of the Continental Army who served mostly in the Northern Theater during the American Revolution. He was lost to history until his detailed memoir from 1830 was rediscovered in the 1950s, providing a priceless primary source for the day-to-day experiences of the common soldier.

Martin was born on November 21, 1760, in Becket, Massachusetts, the son of Reverend Ebenezer Martin and his wife, Susannah (née Plumb) Martin. His father was Yale-educated and from a well-to-do family.

When young Joseph was seven years old, he was sent to live in Milford, Connecticut, with his affluent grandparents. Milford was ninety miles south of Becket, on the Long Island Sound. Here, Martin received a well-rounded education, including reading and writing.

On April 19, 1775, the Battle of Lexington and Concord occurred near Boston, Massachusetts, harkening "The Shot Heard 'Round the World." Young Joseph, approaching his 15th birthday, wanted to fight with the rebels, but his grandparents resisted the idea. When Joseph threatened to run away and join an American privateer to fight the British Navy, they relented and allowed him to join the Connecticut Militia. He enlisted in June 1776, aged fifteen, as a private.

Martin's first tour of duty took him to the New York City area, serving under George Washington, at the start of the British Long Island Campaign. This was disastrous for the Americans, highlighted by Washington's escape across the East River to Manhattan in the fog on August 19, 1776. Martin participated in the Battles of Harlem Heights and White Plains before his tour ended in December 1776, just before Washington's crossing of the Delaware River and the Battles of Trenton and Princeton. Instead,

Joseph Plumb Martin photograph

Martin returned to his grandparents in Connecticut.

The following spring, still itching to join the fight, Martin joined the Continental Army on April 22, 1777, and served until the end of the war. He was initially assigned to the 17th Continental Regiment, formerly the 8th Connecticut Regiment, under Brigadier General James Mitchell Varnum.

In 1777, Martin participated in the Siege of Fort Mifflin near Philadelphia and the Battle of Germantown prior to encamping at Valley Forge for the winter.

The following year, Martin was assigned to the Light Infantry and was promoted to corporal. He participated in the Battle of Monmouth that summer.

In 1779, Martin camped with Washington at Morristown. During the summer of 1780, Martin was promoted to sergeant and was assigned to the Corps of Sappers and Miners upon recommendation from his superior officers. He then witnessed John André being escorted to his execution that fall.

At the decisive Battle of Yorktown during the fall of 1781, Martin's unit was the vanguard for Alexander Hamilton's regiment, digging parallel entrenchments and clearing the field of defenses before Hamilton's capture of Redoubt #10. Martin's account of the action:

At dark the detachment was formed and advanced beyond the trenches and lay down on the ground to await the signal for advancing to the attack, which was to be three shells from a certain battery near where we were lying. All the batteries in our line were silent, and we lay anxiously waiting for the signal. The two brilliant planets, Jupiter and Venus, were in close contact in the western hemisphere, the same direction that the signal was to be made in. When I happened to cast my

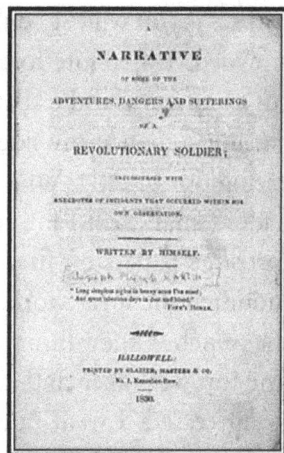

Martin's memoir

eyes to that quarter, which was often, and I caught a glance of them, I was ready to spring on my feet, thinking they were the signal for starting. Our watchword was "Rochambeau," the commander of the French forces' name, a good watchword, for being pronounced Ro-sham-bow, it sounded, when pronounced quick, like rush-on-boys.

We had not lain here long before the expected signal was given, for us and the French, who were to storm the other redoubt, by the three shells with their fiery trains mounting the air in quick succession. The word up, up, was then reiterated through the detachment. We immediately moved silently on toward the redoubt we were to attack, with unloaded muskets. Just as we arrived at the abatis, the enemy discovered us and directly opened a sharp fire upon us. We were now at a place where many of our large shells had burst in the ground, making holes sufficient to bury an ox in. The men, having their eyes fixed upon what was transacting before them, were every now and then falling into these holes. I thought the British were killing us off at a great rate. At length, one of the holes happening to pick me up, I found out the mystery of the huge slaughter.

As soon as the firing began, our people began to cry, "The fort's our own!" and it was "Rush on boys." The Sappers and Miners soon cleared a passage for the infantry, who entered it rapidly. Our Miners were ordered not to enter the fort, but there was no stopping them. "We will go," said they. "Then go to the d——— ," said the commanding officer of our corps, "if you will." I could not pass at the entrance we had made, it was so crowded. I therefore forced a passage at a place where I saw our shot had cut away some of the abatis; several others entered at the same place. While passing, a man at my side received a ball in his head and fell under my feet, crying out bitterly. While crossing the trench, the enemy threw hand grenades (small shells) into it. They were so thick that I at first thought them cartridge papers on fire, but was soon undeceived by their cracking. As I mounted the breastwork, I met an old associate hitching himself down into the trench. I knew him by the light of the enemy's musketry, it was so vivid. The fort was taken and all quiet in a very short time. Immediately after the firing ceased, I went out to see what had become of my wounded friend and the other that fell in the passage. They were both dead. In the heat of the action, I saw a British soldier jump over the walls of the fort next to the river and go down the bank, which was almost perpendicular and twenty or thirty feet high. When he came to the beach he made off for the town, and if he did not make good use of his legs, I never saw a man that did.

Following the victory at Yorktown, Martin accompanied Washington's army back to New York and was discharged in June 1783, before the British evacuated and the Continental Army mustered out that fall.

Next, Martin taught school in New York before settling on Maine's frontier as one of the founders of the town of Prospect, near modern-day Stockton Springs. There, in 1794, he married Lucy Clewley (born 1776). The couple had five children, including Joseph, born 1799; Nathan and Thomas, twins born 1803; James Sullivan, born 1810; and Susan, born 1812.

Also in 1794, Martin's modest 100-acre farm was embroiled in a dispute with former Major General Henry Knox, who as a land speculator, claiming 600,000 acres in what is now known as Waldo County, Maine. Martin's farm was within this claim, and Martin sued to be able to farm his land.

In 1797, Knox's claim was upheld, and Martin's land was appraised at $170, payable over six years in three installments of either cash or farm products. Martin had no money and begged Knox to keep the land, but the general ignored him. However, there is no record of Knox even responding to Martin, and Martin stayed on his land, farming only eight acres.

Over the years, Martin became well-known locally as a farmer, selectman, justice of the peace, and town clerk, a role he held for over twenty-five years.

General Knox died in 1806 and never demanded payment from Martin. However, by 1811, his farmland was reduced to fifty acres and then to nothing in 1818, when he appeared in Massachusetts General Court with other veterans seeking his pension. Martin then received $96 per year for the rest of his life.

Knowing other veterans were having difficulty achieving their pensions, as the nation passed its fiftieth birthday since the Declaration of Independence, Martin began writing about his experiences to call attention to their service. He had written stories and poems over the years, but in 1830, he completed a memoir based on his now-lost journals. This memoir, entitled *A Narrative of Some of the Adventures, Dangers, and Sufferings of a Revolutionary Soldier, Interspersed with Anecdotes of Incidents that Occurred Within His Own Observations*, was published anonymously in Hallowell, Maine, but received little attention. In 1835, the Federal government began offering pensions to enlisted soldiers or their surviving families.

In 1836, on the sixtieth anniversary, a platoon of United States Light Infantry, passing through Prospect, Maine, learned of Plumb and his location. They stopped outside his house and fired a salute in honor of the seventy-five-year-old veteran.

Martin died on May 2, 1850, at age 89. He was buried at the Sandy Point Cemetery, near Stockton Springs, Maine, next to his wife.

In the 1950s, a copy of Martin's book was donated to the Morristown National Historical Park. Little, Brown then published a new edition in 1962 under the title *Private Yankee Doodle*. Other editions have followed with various introductions and forewords by famous historians.

Often cited by scholars and used by re-enactors, Martin's memoir is also critiqued for potential bias or embellishment. However, he does convey in detail the daily experiences of the common soldiers, especially at difficult times such as the winter at Valley Forge.

Martin has since been portrayed in various television documentaries about the American Revolution. Copies of his first edition book reside at the Library of Congress, the US Army Military History Institute at Carlisle, Pennsylvania, and at the Morristown National Historical Park. The Valley Forge National Historical Park has a trail named in his honor that encircles the park.

Martin's grave

Israel Putnam
(1718–1790)

Old Put

Buried at Putnam Monument,
Brooklyn, Connecticut.

———◆———

Military

Israel Putnam, known as "Old Put" to many, was a general in the Continental Army during the American Revolution. Though aggressive and courageous, many questioned his military acumen. He first served notably during the French and Indian War as an officer in Rogers' Rangers. During the Revolution, he was most famous for his service at Bunker Hill, where he is credited with ordering, "Don't fire until you see the whites of their eyes!"

———◆———

Israel Putnam was born in Salem Village (now Danvers), Massachusetts, on January 7, 1718, the son of Joseph Putnam and his wife, Elizabeth (née Porter) Putnam. The Putnams were Puritans and successful farmers. Young Israel was named for his maternal grandfather, Israel Porter, who, along with his son-in-law, Joseph Putnam, challenged local authorities during the Salem Witch Trials in the 1690s. The two men intervened on behalf of Rebecca Nurse, who had been accused of witchcraft. Porter and Putnam signed a petition on her behalf, and she was initially found innocent. However, a jury overturned the ruling, and Nurse was convicted and executed. Her sister was also executed during the craze.

Regarding Putnam's upbringing, historian Benson J. Lossing wrote in 1869, "His education was neglected, and he grew to manhood with a

Israel Putnam

vigorous but uncultivated mind." In 1738/39, Putnam married his first wife, Hannah Pope. She was the mother of his ten children. The young family moved to northeastern Connecticut to Mortlake, later part of Pomfret and Brooklyn. There, Putnam became a prosperous farmer.

As a young farmer in 1743, Putnam became a local hero when he killed a wolf that had been menacing his sheep and those of his neighbors. They had tracked the she-wolf to its lair, but their dogs would go no further, some of them injured by the wolf. They attempted to smoke the wolf out of its den using sulfur, but this was to no avail. None of the farmers were willing to enter the cave, and Putnam's servant was likewise inclined to stay out, despite him being handed a torch and gun and ordered to do so. At wit's end, Putnam grabbed the torch and his musket loaded with buckshot and crawled into the cave with a rope around his waist in case he needed to be pulled out quickly. He crawled inside about forty feet, down the narrow passageway, until he saw glowing red eyes and heard the snarl of the beast. He then shot the wolf, killing it, and dragged it out by its ears. The farmers were so delighted; they carried Putnam through the village in a torchlit parade that went late into the night. The nicknames "Wolf Putnam" and "Old Wolf Put" stuck with Putnam for many years afterward. Today in Pomfret, Connecticut, there is a section of Mashamoquet Brook State Park named "Wolf Den," believed to be the event's site.

At age 37, in 1755, after Braddock's defeat, Putnam was summoned into the Connecticut militia and quickly moved up the ranks from private to second lieutenant, captain, major, lieutenant colonel, and colonel. He had natural leadership abilities and charisma and excelled at recruiting men into his regiment. When a captain, Putnam was introduced to Major Robert Rogers, with whom he served in the upcoming expedition to Crown Point, establishing a reputation as a capable frontier fighter. It was said that "Rogers always sent, but Putnam led his men to action."

By 1757, Putnam had seen action at Fort William Henry and was promoted to major. In February 1758, at Fort Edward, along the Hudson River near modern-day Glens Falls, New York, Putnam again exhibited great courage and personal sacrifice. A fire broke out in the barracks near the gunpowder. Fearing an explosion, Putnam got up on the roof and poured bucket after bucket of water on the flames, getting down only when the fire was within feet of the magazine. He then continued to fight the fire until it was extinguished, receiving severe burns and blisters that sidelined him for several weeks.

Putnam was back in action with Rogers' Rangers at the Battle of Fort Carillon, also known as the 1758 Battle of Ticonderoga, on July 8, 1758. He led a regiment into the Valley of Death. Ultimately, the British attack failed, and the French held the fort.

Near Fort Miller on the Hudson, Putnam was alone in a batteau when he was surprised by Indians. He then shot the rapids in his boat, astonishing the natives. After a fierce skirmish near Fort Ann, New York,

Major Putnam was captured by Mohawk Indians on August 8, 1758. They stripped him and tied him to a tree, intending to burn him alive. An early biographer described the natives as they howled and danced around the encroaching flames. Putnam believed his life was at an end and thought of his dear family. Suddenly, a French officer burst through the woods and intervened. He untied Putnam and took him into captivity. After the British victory at Fort Frontenac, later that month, Putnam was exchanged for French prisoners. He was promoted to lieutenant colonel soon after that.

By 1760, the tide had turned in favor of the British. In General Jeffrey Amherst's campaign to successfully take Canada at Oswegatchie, New York, Putnam captured two French ships, boarding them after approaching them in shallow rowboats. As Canada was surrendered to the English, it appeared Putnam's role in the war was at an end. However, after Spain invaded Britain's ally Portugal in May 1762, Putnam took part in an expedition against Havana, Cuba, then a Spanish territory, and was shipwrecked. Not deterred, the assault was successful. Putnam is said to have brought back Cuban tobacco seeds, which he planted in Connecticut, later leading to the Connecticut Wrapper cigar's creation.

During Pontiac's Rebellion, Putnam took up arms again as part of the relief expedition to Detroit in 1764. After the campaign, Putnam returned to civilian life. He joined the Congregational Church in his town.

In 1765, Hannah Putnam died, leaving Putnam a widower alone with ten children. This did not deter him from his public life. Now the owner of a tavern, he became involved in politics. During the Stamp Act crisis of 1765 and 1766, Putnam was vocal against the tax. Putnam was elected to the Connecticut General Assembly and was one of the founders of the local Sons of Liberty. In 1767, he married his second wife, Deborah (née Crow) Lothrop, the widow of Samuel Lothrop.

As the hostilities with Britain began to ramp up, Putnam headed the local Committee of Correspondence in 1774. He was also made a lieutenant colonel in the Connecticut militia. After the British closed the port of Boston, Putnam drove a herd of sheep to the city to benefit the locals. The day after the fighting began the following April at Lexington and Concord, Putnam plowed a field with his son. Upon hearing the news, he unhitched his team, sent word for his regiment to gather, and rode off to the action without changing his clothes. Putnam rode 100 miles in eight hours, arriving in Cambridge the next day. He was named a major general, second in rank to only Artemas Ward, head of the Army of Observation, the Continental Army's precursor. Putnam gathered his troops and conducted numerous sorties against the British, ranging from taunting the British from Charlestown to burning a beached warship. Putnam's goal was to keep his men sharp, anticipating a significant engagement. While discussing the upcoming battle with Joseph Warren and Artemas Ward, Ward suggested a defensive posture, "As peace and reconciliation is what we seek for, would it not be better to act only on the defensive and give no unnecessary provocation?" Putnam, irked by this, turned to Warren and exclaimed, "You know, Dr. Warren, we shall have no peace worth anything till we gain it by the sword!"

While the British troops readied in Boston to attack the colonials at Bunker Hill, Putnam also argued to fortify the adjacent Breed's Hill, closer to Boston. From this point, cannons could threaten the British there, forcing them to attack the hill. Throughout the morning of June 17, 1775, General William Howe began massing roughly 2,300 British troops near Charlestown to attack the freshly dug American defenses. Meanwhile, with Breed's Hill set, Putnam reinforced the forces at Bunker Hill. General Howe ordered the attack at 3:30 PM. Putnam left Bunker Hill to join General William Prescott on Breed's Hill. It is here that Putnam may have ordered Prescott to tell his troops, "Don't fire until you see the whites of their eyes." While it is debated who said these words, the point was to be careful with the precious stock of ammunition.

As the British approached, they were cut down. Putnam rode through the American lines, encouraging his men to hold their positions. Eventually, the Americans ran out of powder and had to retreat. Putnam rallied his Connecticut troops at Winter Hill to make another stand. However, the British stopped their advance. In the end, the tally at Bunker/Breed's Hill was 1054 British casualties, to 449 for the colonials. Wrote General Nathanael Greene to his brother, "I wish we could sell them another hill, at the same price."

On June 14, 1775, before the battle, and unknown to those involved, the Continental Congress voted unanimously for George Washington to be Commander-in-Chief of the army. Putnam was retained as one of the four major generals, the only one to receive a unanimous vote like Washington. Historian Richard Ketchum wrote, "Putnam was five feet six inches tall, powerfully built, and had the face of a cherubic bulldog mounted on a jaw cut like a block of wood." He was regarded as a great soldier based on his reputation during the French and Indian War. Ketchum suggests he was not skilled enough to be a major general, lacking a strategic purview.

Washington placed Putnam in charge of the reserve division for the remainder of the Siege of Boston. Around this time, Washington discussed the siege at length with his officers. Putnam grew tired of all the talk and walked to a window to observe the British. Washington, who noticed Putnam's absence, beckoned him to return. Putnam responded, "Oh, my dear General, you may plan the battle to suit yourself, and I will fight it."

On another occasion, while dining with his fellow officers, Washington offered a toast for "A speedy and honorable peace." A few days later, Putnam offered a contrarian toast for "A long and moderate war." This prompted a laugh from Washington who said to Putnam, "You are the last man, General Putnam, from whom I should have expected such a toast, you who are always urging vigorous measures, to plead now for a long, and what is still more extraordinary, a moderate, war, seems strange indeed." Putnam explained a short war would lead to a divisive false peace. He said, "I expect nothing but a long war, and I would have it a moderate one, that we may hold out till the mother country becomes willing to cast us off forever."

Ultimately, thanks to Henry Knox and Putnam's cousin Rufus Putnam, the British were forced to abandon Boston. At this point, the focus of the war shifted to New York. Putnam was in temporary command of forces there until Washington arrived on April 13, 1776. At Long Island in August 1776, Putnam set the defenses at Guana Heights. General Howe's forces easily outflanked them. The Continental Congress blamed Putnam for the defeat, but Washington did not. Senator Daniel Patrick Moynihan described Putnam's importance, ". . . it could be argued that we owe our national existence to the fortifications which General Israel Putnam threw up in April 1776 on the Buttermilk Channel side [of

Governors Island, New York] . . . [British troops] landed on Long Island and headed for George Washington and his army. He had to flee, and he made it because Putnam's artillery firing on Brooklyn Heights, over the Buttermilk Channel, held Howe back just long enough for Washington to escape to Manhattan and for the Revolutionary War to proceed."

After Long Island, Putnam returned to the Hudson Valley he was familiar with from his earlier days. In October 1777, Putnam was fooled by a feint by General Sir Henry Clinton, which led to Clinton's capture of Fort Montgomery and Fort Clinton on the Hudson. Putnam was brought before a court of inquiry, but it was determined the losses were due to a lack of men and not the commander's fault.

Putnam was not without his controversies. He was known to show favor to captured British officers, especially former comrades. He offered them newspapers and medical attention. He was also against the sale of Tory property, referring to it as embezzlement. This angered many New Yorkers involved in the practice. Washington lost faith in Putnam when he delayed sending troops as ordered. However, this happened around the time word came that Deborah Putnam had been mistaken for dead and buried alive. The casket was exhumed to reveal the error, too late. Washington decided to move Putnam closer to home and gave him recruiting duties in Connecticut and New Hampshire.

During the winter of 1778-1779, Putnam was encamped near Redding, Connecticut, a site now preserved as Putnam Memorial State Park. Here, on February 26, 1779, he was nearly captured by the British. To escape, he rode down a steep slope. A statue of Putnam was erected near this spot. By 1779, Putnam oversaw the troops from Virginia, Maryland, and Pennsylvania. But in December, while riding home to Connecticut, he suffered a stroke, which affected his speech and mobility.

Israel Putnam lingered, incapacitated, for over ten years, succumbing on May 29, 1790. He was buried in the South Cemetery in Brooklyn, Connecticut, in an above-ground tomb. However, over the years, souvenir hunters chipped away at it, making it unfit. An equestrian statue was erected in the town square in 1888, and Putnam's remains were re-interred beneath it.

A captured Hessian once said of Putnam, "This old gray-beard may be a good honest man, but nobody but the rebels would have made him a general." Wrote historian Nathaniel Philbrick, "Israel Putnam was the provincial army's most beloved officer."

Israel Putnam is remembered in many ways with statues, paintings, and historic sites. Nine counties in various states are named after him, as are several towns and many streets.

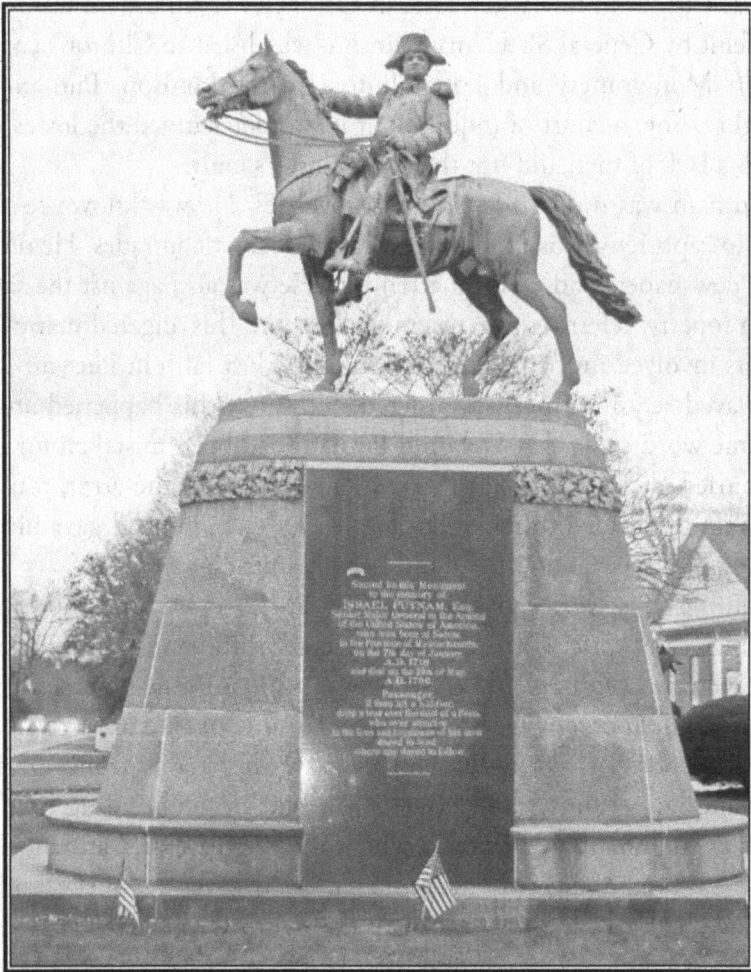

Impressive equestrian memorial and grave for Ol' Put

Roger Sherman
(1721 – 1793)

Three-Fifths Compromise

Buried at Grove Street Cemetery,
New Haven, Connecticut.

———◆•◆———

**Continental Association • Declaration of Independence
Articles of Confederation • U.S. Constitution**

Roger Sherman, of Connecticut, was the only person to sign all four founding documents of the United States of America: Continental Association, Declaration of Independence, Articles of Confederation, and Constitution. A lawyer and statesman, he with James Wilson proposed the Three-Fifths Compromise during the Constitutional Convention. Sherman later served as a member of the U.S. House of Representatives and as a U.S. Senator.

———◆•◆———

Sherman was born in Newton, Massachusetts, on April 19, 1721, to William Sherman and his second wife Mehetabel (née Wellington) Sherman. Others in his family tree include Senator, Secretary of the Treasury, and Secretary of State John Sherman (1823-1900), Civil War General William Tecumseh Sherman (1820-1891), and Senator William Maxwell Evarts (1818-1901), who was also Attorney General and Secretary of State.

William Sherman was variously a cordwainer, farmer, and shoemaker in Stoughton, Massachusetts. He married first Rebecca Cutler of Watertown with whom he had a son, William, who died in infancy.

Portrait of Roger Sherman by Ralph Earl, circa 1776

He then married Mehetabel Wellington of Watertown on September 3, 1715. Roger was born in 1721 and lived on the farm in Stoughton until 1743, studying his father's trades and never receiving a formal education. From pastor Reverend Samuel Dunbar, Roger privately learned the classics and theology. When William Sherman died in 1741, 18-year-old Roger cared for his widowed mother and the rest of the family.

In 1743, Roger literally followed in his older brother William's footsteps, setting out on foot with his cobbler's tools to find work in New Milford, Connecticut. Soon, a local attorney took notice of his writing ability and urged him to become a lawyer. In 1745, Sherman was named the surveyor of New Haven County, remaining in that position until 1752, after which he was the surveyor for Litchfield County until 1758. During this time, he turned his earnings and observations into great wealth through well-played land speculation.

Sherman married Elizabeth Hartwell of Stoughton, Massachusetts, in November 1749. The two had seven children, four of whom lived to adulthood. After Elizabeth passed in 1760 at the age of 34, Sherman moved to New Haven and married Rebecca Prescott in May 1763. The couple had eight children, seven of whom lived to adulthood.

Beginning in 1750, like Benjamin Franklin, Sherman began publishing a series of almanacs on a variety of subjects expressing his ideas and showcasing his writing ability. He studied law and was admitted to the Connecticut colonial bar in 1754. In 1755, he was elected to the Connecticut colonial Assembly, serving until 1766. He was also a justice of the peace for Litchfield County from 1755 to 1761. Later, he served in the state Senate (1766-1785), and as a judge of the Superior Court (1766-67 and 1773-88).

Beginning in the mid-1760s, Sherman was a leader in opposition to the British Parliament, personally urging protest of The Stamp Act. Though he was not initially one of the radical Sons of Liberty, he did eventually join the Committee of Correspondence to communicate with the other colonies following the Boston Tea Party.

As royal rule collapsed in Connecticut, Jonathan Trumbull was named the governor. He was a friend of Sherman's and named him one of 12 assistants including Eliphalet Dyer and William Samuel Johnson. For the first Continental Congress in 1774, Connecticut sent Sherman, Dyer, and Silas Deane.

In Philadelphia, Silas Deane was not impressed with his fellow delegate, writing in a letter to his wife, "Mr. Sherman is clever in private, but I will only say he is as badly calculated to appear in such Company as a chestnut-burr is for an eye-stone. He occasioned some shrewd countenances among the company, and not a few oaths, by the odd questions he asked, and the very odd and countrified cadence with which he speaks; but he was, and did, as well as I expected."

Sherman served in the Continental Congress from 1774 to 1781 and then again in 1784 during which he did more than Jefferson, or Adams, or any other delegate, signing the Continental Association, the Olive Branch Petition, the Declaration of Independence, the Articles of Confederation, and, eventually, as a delegate to the Constitutional Convention, the U.S. Constitution. He also wrote hundreds of letters, documents, and other correspondence "to establish regulations and restrictions on the trade of the United States; to regulate the currency of

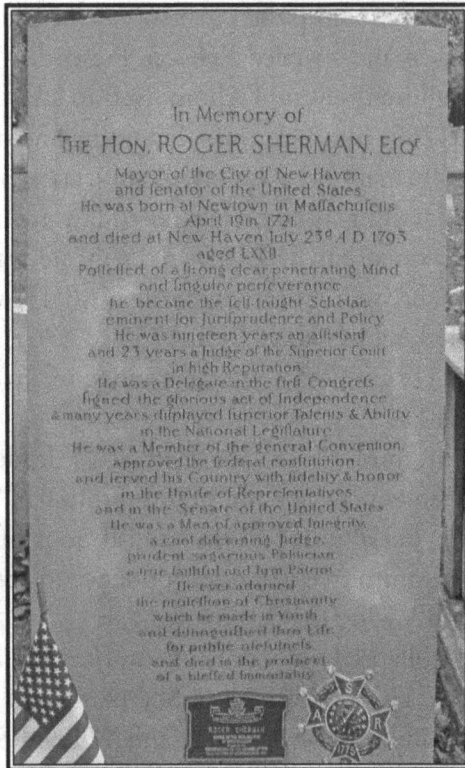

In Memory of
THE HON. ROGER SHERMAN, Esq.
Mayor of the City of New Haven
and Senator of the United States
He was born at Newtown in Massachusetts
April 19th 1721.
and died at New Haven July 23d A D 1793
aged LXXII

Grave of Roger Sherman at Grove Street Cemetery
in New Haven, Connecticut (photo by Lawrence
Knorr)

the country; to furnish supplies for the army; to provide for the expenses
of the government; to prepare articles of confederation between the several states; and to propose a plan of military operations for the campaign
of 1776."

Roger Sherman's biggest contribution in the Continental Congress
may have been on June 11, 1776, when he was named to the committee
to draft a declaration of independence from England along with Thomas
Jefferson, John Adams, Benjamin Franklin, and Robert Livingston.

After the Revolution, Sherman was selected to represent Connecticut
at the Constitutional Convention. He again played a prominent role as
a key player in many votes. After the ratification of the Constitution,
Sherman was elected to the First Congress (1789-1791). However, he

did not quite finish his term, instead taking the vacant Senate seat of William Samuel Johnson on March 4, 1791.

In 1987, a draft of the Bill of Rights was found among James Madison's papers at the Library of Congress written in Sherman's hand. Historians have argued since over whether Sherman was a collaborator with Madison, or just made a copy for the record. According to Christopher Collier, the former Connecticut State Historian, Sherman was simply making a copy. He had been against a Bill of Rights even after the draft was recorded.

Sherman served as a senator until his death at home in New Haven on July 23, 1793. He was 72. Sherman was buried at the New Haven Green. A few years after his death, a new cemetery was started a few blocks away to deal with the overcrowding under the Green. By 1821, many of the families had moved their loved ones' graves and headstones to the new cemetery. However, for thousands, this was not done. Only the headstones were moved, but the remains were not. Thus, perhaps 5,000 to 10,000 people remain buried under the New Haven Green. We believe some or all of Roger Sherman was moved to Grove Street Cemetery.

Noah Webster
(1758–1843)

Man of Many Words

Buried at Grove Street Cemetery,
New Haven, Connecticut.

————◆◆◆————

Thought Leader

Although Noah Webster hasn't uttered a syllable since his death on May 28, 1843, to this day many people still introduce the definition of a word with the phrase "Webster says." As a matter of fact, Webster's fame and name have become so associated with "dictionary" that his other accomplishments have been overshadowed by the creation that still bears his name. In 2006, John Morse, president, and publisher of Merriam-Webster, Inc. noted that because of his work as a dictionary maker Webster "is probably one of the least known of the Founding Fathers." Morse also pointed out that Webster was one of the most influential thinkers in the period leading up to the 1787 Constitutional Convention saying, "Just about every delegate had read his 1785 tract *Sketches on American Policy* and was influenced by it." Among the recommendations in the work was the establishment of a constitutional government that included a Congress.

————◆◆◆————

Noah Webster was born on October 16, 1758, in West Hartford, Connecticut. His father was a descendant of John Webster a former Connecticut Governor and his mother was a descendant of William Bradford who was Governor of the Plymouth Colony. Webster attended

Portrait of Noah Webster by Samuel Finley Breese Morse

school in a one-room schoolhouse. He would later describe the teachers there as the "dregs of humanity" and this early experience with education would serve to inspire and motivate him to improve the educational opportunities for the generations that would follow him.

Webster enrolled at Yale College shortly before he turned 16. His four years at Yale coincided with the American Revolution and the young student served in the Connecticut militia. After graduation, he studied law under a future United States Supreme Court Chief justice Oliver Ellsworth. During this period, he was also teaching school full time, a schedule he found impossible to manage, so he abandoned the study of law for a year and did not pass the bar examination until 1781.

It was around this time that Webster turned his attention to writing for a New England newspaper. His stories championed the Revolution and set forth the argument that the American separation from England was permanent. His work brought him to the attention of many prominent Americans including George Washington and Benjamin Franklin. These and other American leaders corresponded with Webster sharing ideas on the new nation. Years before these leaders met to form a new United States government Webster wrote: "So long as any individual state has power to defeat the measures of the other twelve, our pretended union is but a name, and our confederation, a cobweb."

When the Philadelphia Convention sent the Constitution to the states for ratification, Webster became an ardent supporter of the document. In 1787 he wrote a pamphlet titled *An Examination into the Leading Principles of the Federal Constitution Proposed by the Late Convention Held at Philadelphia*. His arguments favoring ratification proved influential throughout the states. He also expressed his feelings on the first ten amendments to the Constitution, the Bill of Rights, when he wrote: "paper declarations of rights are trifling things and no real security to liberty." His thoughts on the subject reflected the feelings of many other Founders including Richard Henry Lee and Elbridge Gerry.

Webster married Rebecca Greenleaf in 1789 and the couple would produce eight children. The family would eventually settle in New Haven, Connecticut where Webster would aid in the founding of Amherst College. Webster's marriage followed a series of failures in the romantic realm at least one of which led to a depressive state that he worked himself out of through his writing.

Alexander Hamilton lent Webster $1,500 in 1793 so he could move to New York City to edit the leading Federalist newspaper that supported the policies proposed by the Washington Administration. In this role, he was repeatedly criticized by the supporters of Thomas Jefferson who referred to him as "a deceitful newsmonger" and "an incurable lunatic." He also endured critics among fellow Federalists who accused him of harboring pro-French views. While it was true that Webster was influenced by the French theorist Jean-Jacques Rousseau, he also urged that the United States remain neutral when war broke out between England and France in 1793. He also opposed the French foreign minister Citizen Genet for setting up clubs or societies whose purpose was to attack President Washington's neutrality proclamation. Webster advised his fellow Federalist writers to ignore the clubs. He predicted that peace would render them obsolete.

With time, Webster's influence as a Founder was overshadowed by his contributions to American education. His three-volume work titled *A Grammatical Institute of the English Language* included the Webster speller which taught children in America to read, spell, and pronounce words for generations. Referred to by most as the "Blue-Backed Speller," by 1890 its sales totaled 60 million. His dictionary, first published in 1806 though not completed until 1825, contained seventy thousand words and twelve thousand of these had never before appeared in such a work. In May of 1843, he completed work on revising the appendix to the dictionary's second edition. A few days later, on the 23rd of the month at the age of 84, he passed away. He was laid to rest in the Grove Street Cemetery in New Haven.

Grave of Noah Webster at Grove Street Cemetery in New Haven, Connecticut (photo by Lawrence Knorr)

Noah Webster is certainly not forgotten largely due to his work on the dictionary that still bears his name. The same cannot be said for his work as one of the nation's Founders given his influence on the thinking of men like Franklin, Washington, and James Madison. Indeed, one could argue that Madison would not have been off-base had he begun some of the arguments he made at the Constitutional Convention with the words "Webster says."

William Williams
(1731–1811)

Puritan Patriot

Buried at Trumbull Cemetery,
Lebanon, Connecticut.

Declaration of Independence

William Williams was a soldier in the French and Indian War, a merchant, local and state government official, and son-in-law of Connecticut royal governor Jonathan Trumbull, the only governor to convert to the patriot cause. Williams was appointed to the Second Continental Congress, where he signed the Declaration of Independence.

William Williams was born March 29, 1731, in Lebanon, Connecticut, to First Congregational Church minister Solomon Williams and his wife Mary (née Porter). After attending local preparatory schools, Williams entered Harvard College at 16, where he studied theology and law, graduating in 1751.

At the age of 21, Williams was elected to the office of town clerk in Lebanon and later town treasurer. He served as town clerk for 44 years. While performing these duties, Williams planned to become a minister and studied with his father. He was ordained a deacon in his father's church. Yale College awarded Williams a bachelor's degree in 1753 for his previous work at Harvard. Williams then completed a master's degree at Harvard in 1754.

On the verge of becoming a minister, Williams heard the call to arms at the outset of the French and Indian War. He served as an aide under his

William Williams

older cousin, Colonel Ephraim Williams, from Massachusetts, who led ten companies of William Johnson's expedition against the French fort at Crown Point, New York. During the expedition, Johnson renamed *Lac du Saint-Sacrement* to Lake George in honor of his king. During the Battle of Lake George on September 8, 1755, Colonel Ephraim Williams was shot in the head and killed by an ambush of French soldiers and allied Indians. This incident became known as the Bloody Morning Scout. The colonel's body was hidden by his regiment to prevent its desecration. He was then buried nearby, and a stone with his initials and year of death stands at Lake George near a monument erected in his honor. The assets of the colonel's estate were subsequently used to establish Williamstown,

Massachusetts, and Williams College. In the early 20th century, the colonel's body was disinterred at Lake George and moved to the chapel at Williams College. The alumni also funded the monument at Lake George, marking the site of the ambush.

Though the British ultimately won the battle and erected Fort William Henry on the shores of Lake George, this experience caused William Williams to begin to question his loyalty to them. He did not like how the provincials, including his cousin, were treated as inferiors. He began to think the colonies might do better to govern themselves.

After Lake George, Williams returned to Lebanon and opened a retail store called The Williams, Inc. However, politics soon called, and he was elected to the Connecticut General Assembly in 1757, serving until May 4, 1776, when he was promoted to the upper house known as the Council of Assistants. Having left his business behind, Williams was so passionate about his public service, he never missed a session. In addition to his role in the assembly, Williams was a member of the Sons of Liberty and later served on the Committee of Correspondence and Council of Safety in Connecticut. When British soldiers occupied Boston in 1768, Williams voiced his opposition. When the British implemented the Townshend Acts in 1769, Williams strongly opposed them and was a staunch supporter of the colonials' non-importation agreements. When the British repealed the Townshend Acts in 1770, except for the tax on tea, Williams urged merchants to continue to adhere to the non-importation agreements. However, few listened, including Silas Deane, whom Williams never trusted.

Finally, at the age of 40, Williams set aside his duties to marry Mary Trumbull on Valentine's Day, February 14, 1771. Mary was the daughter of Connecticut Royal Governor Jonathan Trumbull, who had also previously struggled at being a merchant. The couple ultimately produced three children: Solomon, born 1772; Faith, 1774; and William Trumbull, 1777. The marriage forged a strong bond between Williams and his father-in-law, who was also a native of Lebanon, Connecticut.

Following the Boston Tea Party, the British parliament implemented the Coercive Acts in 1774. On July 1 of that year, Williams published a satirical address to the king in the *Connecticut Gazette* under a pseudonym. Wrote Williams:

We don't complain that your father made our yoke heavy and afflicted us with grievous service. We only ask that you would govern us upon the same constitutional plan, and with the same justice and moderation that he did, and we will serve you forever. And what is the language of your answer . . . ? Ye Rebels and Traitors . . . if ye don't yield implicit obedience to all my commands, just and unjust, ye shall be drag'd in chains across the wide ocean, to answer your insolence, and if a mob arises among you to impede my officers in the execution of my orders, I will punish and involve in common ruin whole cities and colonies, with their ten thousand innocents, and ye shan't be heard in your own defense, but shall be murdered and butchered by my dragoons into silence and submission. Ye reptiles! ye are scarce intitled [sic] to existence any longer . . . Your lives, liberties, and property are all at the absolute disposal of my parliament.

Williams not only voiced his concerns, he invested over two thousand dollars of his own money in continental currency to support the rebellion. He used his connections as a former merchant to collect blankets and munitions for the cause. He assisted his father-in-law, who was the only royal governor to join the patriots, in preparing to establish the new rebel government in Connecticut. In 1775, Williams was elected speaker of the Connecticut Assembly and then to the Continental Congress to replace Oliver Wolcott on July 11, 1776. That day, word was received of the vote for independence on July 2, nine days prior. Williams hurried to Philadelphia, arriving on July 28. While he was too late to vote for the Declaration of Independence, he signed the document as a representative of Connecticut.

Some have written about Williams's self-righteous attitude. Perhaps he was overly confident as the son-in-law of the governor. In one exchange at a Council of Safety meeting in late 1776, when it looked like the British might prevail, Williams said calmly, "If they succeed, it is pretty evident what will be my fate. I have done much to prosecute the contest, and one thing I have done which the British will never pardon, I have signed the Declaration of Independence." To that, Congressman

Benjamin Huntington replied he should be exempt from the gallows because he had not signed the document. Williams retorted, "Then sir, you deserve to be hanged for not having done your duty."

Williams, a man of devout faith, was also somewhat puritanical. In a letter to his father-in-law, the governor, regarding the celebration of the first anniversary of the Declaration of Independence, he wrote:

> Yesterday was, in my opinion, poorly spent in celebrating the anniversary of the Declaration of Independence. But to avoid singularity and Reflection upon my dear colony, I thot my duty to attend the public entertainment; a great expenditure of Liquor, Powder, etc. took up a good part of the Day and of candles thro the City, good part of the night.

After 1777, Williams returned to Connecticut and continued his public service. He was a judge of the Windham County Court from 1776 to 1804 and Windham district probate judge from 1776 to 1808. He became an assistant councilor in 1780 and served as assistant and as councilor for 24 years. He returned to the state house of representatives from 1780 to 1784 and was the speaker from 1781 to 1783. In 1787, Williams was a member of the ratification convention in Connecticut for the new U.S. Constitution. At the state's constitutional convention in 1788, Williams represented Lebanon. His only objection was a clause banning religious tests for government officials.

Under the new constitution, brother-in-law Jonathan Trumbull, Jr. was elected to the first three U.S. congresses from 1789 through 1795. During the Second Congress, he was Speaker of the House, sandwiched between two terms when Frederick Muhlenberg had the role. Trumbull was then governor of Connecticut from 1798 to 1809. Another brother-in-law, John Trumbull, was known as the "painter of the American Revolution."

During his later years, Williams was a pastor at the First Congregational Church in Lebanon and a successful merchant. He spent the last years of his life devoted to reading, meditation, and prayer. On August 2, 1811, he died at Lebanon and was interred in the Trumbull Tomb in the East

Cemetery in the town, now known as Trumbull Cemetery. His house still stands and is on the National Registry of Historic Landmarks.

The grave of William Williams

Oliver Wolcott
(1726 – 1797)

Connecticut Yankee

Buried at East Cemetery
Litchfield, Connecticut

———————

Declaration of Independence • Articles of Confederation

Oliver Wolcott was a Revolutionary War hero who went on to serve as a member of the Continental Congress and sign the Declaration of Independence and later the Articles of Confederation. He commanded fourteen regiments of troops during the Revolutionary War and rose to the rank of Major General. He served for ten years as Connecticut's Lieutenant Governor beginning in 1786 and in 1796 became Governor until he died in 1797.

———————

Wolcott was born in Windsor, Connecticut on November 20, 1726, the youngest of ten children to Colonial Governor Roger Wolcott and Sarah Drake Wolcott. He attended Yale College and graduated at the top of his class in 1747. Immediately upon graduating, he received a captain's commission from New York Governor George Clinton to fight in King George's War. He served on the northern frontier defending the Canadian border against the French until the Treaty of Aix-La-Chappelle of 1748. After the war, his regiment was disbanded and Wolcott returned to Connecticut to study medicine with his uncle, Dr. Alexander Wolcott. He completed his training but rather than pursue a career in medicine he settled in the newly developed area of Litchfield County where his father

Oliver Wolcott

owned land and pursued an entirely different career. He was elected
sheriff of the county at the age of twenty-five and founded a successful
business. He served as Sheriff from 1751 to 1771. He also represented
Litchfield in both houses of the colonial and state legislatures and later
was appointed as judge of the Litchfield Probate and County Courts.

Wolcott married Lorraine (Laura) Collins, the daughter of a sea captain. The couple had five children, four of whom survived to adulthood.
Wolcott remained active in the militia during the period leading up to
the Revolutionary War, devoting portions of each year to militia duty.
He rose through the ranks, serving as captain and then major in 1771,
and was promoted to colonel in 1774, and later rose to Major General.

As tensions escalated between the colonies and Britain Wolcott became an active participant in the Patriot cause. He was elected to the
Continental Congress in 1775 and was an ardent proponent of independence noting "a final separation between the countries I consider

as unavoidable." The Congress named him a Commissioner of Indian Affairs and asked him to persuade the northern Indian nations to remain neutral. His experience in the French and Indian War led to that assignment.

In the summer of 1776, a brief illness and Wolcott's role in military affairs drew him away from his political responsibilities, resulting in his absence from Congress during the adoption of the Declaration of Independence. When he recovered from his illness, rather than returning to Philadelphia, the Connecticut Governor Jonathan Trumbull appointed him to command a detachment of fourteen regiments of Connecticut militia to defend New York, which he did.

On July 9, he was in New York City when George Washington read the Declaration of Independence to the troops. A demonstration followed and a group of soldiers toppled a large statue of King George III. The statue was made of lead and shattered into many pieces. The head was put on a spike outside a tavern. Wolcott arranged for the collection of the pieces and had them shipped off to the general's house. There, Wolcott, his family, and some local patriots melted the lead and made over 42,000 bullets for the war effort. In October 1777 he used some of these bullets in the defeat of General Burgoyne's troops at Saratoga, New York. The victory was a turning point in the war, bolstering American morale and convincing France to support the revolution.

In the fall of 1776, Wolcott returned to Philadelphia and signed the Declaration of Independence. After the victory at Saratoga Wolcott returned to Congress which was then meeting in York, Pennsylvania due to the British occupation of Philadelphia. There he signed the Articles of Confederation, the nation's first constitution.

In 1786 Wolcott was elected Lieutenant Governor of Connecticut, a post he would hold for ten years. He was a member of the Connecticut State Convention which ratified the Constitution of the United States in 1787. He became governor when Samuel Huntington died on January 5, 1796. He held the office until his own death at age 71. He died on December 1, 1797, and was buried at East Cemetery beside his wife.

Oliver Wolcott Jr, his son, served as Secretary of the Treasury under George Washington and John Adams and as Governor of Connecticut. A plaque commemorating Wolcott signing the Declaration of Independence can be found on the Signers Walk on the six hundred block of Chestnut Street in Philadelphia. His home in Litchfield, Connecticut was declared a National Historic Landmark in 1971. The town of Walcott, Connecticut was named in honor of Oliver and his son.

Wolcott's grave

Sources

Books, Magazines, Journals, Files:

Alexander, Edward P. *Revolutionary Conservative: James Duane of New York.* New York: Ams Press, 1978.

Anthony, Katharine Susan. *First Lady of the Revolution; The Life of Mercy Otis Warren.* Port Washington, N.Y.: Kennikat Press, 1972.

Appleby, Joyce. *Inheriting the Revolution: The First Generation of Americans.* Cambridge, Massachusetts: Harvard University Press, 2000.

Atkinson, Rick. *The British Are Coming: The War for America, Lexington to Princeton, 1775-1777.* New York: Henry Holt & Co. 2019.

Bordewich, Fergus M. *The First Congress: How James Madison, George Washington, and a Group of Extraordinary Men Invented the Government.* New York: Simon and Schuster Paperbacks, 2016.

Boudreau, George W. *Independence: A Guide to Historic Philadelphia.* Yardley, Pennsylvania: Westholme Publishing, LLC. 2012.

Bowen, Catherine Drinker. *Miracle at Philadelphia: The Story of the Constitutional Convention May to September 1787.* Boston, Massachusetts: Little, Brown & Company, 1966.

Breen, T.H, *George Washington's Journey: The President Forges a New Nation.* New York: Simon & Schuster. 2016.

Brookhiser, Richard. *Gentleman Revolutionary: Gouverneur Morris The Rake Who Wrote the Constitution.* New York: Free Press, 2003.

———. *John Marshall: The Man Who Made the Supreme Court.* New York: Basic Books. 2018.

Brush, Edward Hale. *Rufus King and His Times.* New York: N.L. Brown, 1926.

Chadwick, Bruce. I Am Murdered: *George Wythe, Thomas Jefferson, and the Killing That Shocked a New Nation.* Hoboken, New Jersey: John Wiley & Sons, 2009.

Chambers, II, John Whiteclay. *The Oxford Companion to American Military History.* Oxford: Oxford University Press, 1999.

Commager, Henry Steele & Richard B. Morris. *The Spirit of 'Seventy-Six: The Story of the American Revolution as Told by Participants.* New York: Harper & Rowe, 1967.

Cole, Ryan. *Light-Horse Harry Lee: The Rise and Fall of a Revolutionary Hero.* Washington, D.C.: Regnery History. 2019.

Conlin, Joseph R. *The Morrow Book of Quotations in American History.* New York: William Morrow and Company, Inc., 1984.

Daniels, Jonathan. *Ordeal of Ambition.* Garden City, New York: Doubleday & Company, Inc., 1970.

Dann, John C. *The Revolution Remembered: Eyewitness Accounts of the War for Independence.* Chicago: University of Chicago Press, 1980.

DeRose, Chris. *Founding Rivals: Madison vs. Monroe: The Bill of Rights and the Election that Saved a Nation*. New York: MJF Books, 2011.

Drury, Bob & Tom Clavin. *Valley Forge*. New York: Simon & Schuster. 2018.

Ellis, Joseph J. *Revolutionary Summer: The Birth of American Independence*. New York: Alfred A. Knopf, 2013.

———. *The Quartet: Orchestrating the Second American Revolution, 1783-1789*. New York: Alfred A. Knopf, 2015.

———. *His Excellency: George Washington*. New York: Alfred A. Knopf, 2004.

Flexner, James Thomas. *George Washington in the American Revolution, 1775-1783*. Boston: Little, Brown & Company, 1967.

Flower, Lenore Embick. "Visit of President George Washington to Carlisle, 1794." Carlisle, Pennsylvania: The Hamilton Library and Cumberland County Historical Society, 1932.

Gerlach, Don R. *Proud Patriot: Philip Schuyler and the War of Independence, 1775-1783*. Syracuse, N.Y.: Syracuse University Press, 1987.

Goodrich, Charles A. *Lives of the Signers of the Declaration of Independence*. Charlotteville, N.Y.: SamHar Press, 1976.

Griffith, IV, William R. *The Battle of Lake George: England's First Triumph in the French and Indian War*. Charleston, South Carolina: The History Press, 2016.

Grossman, Mark. *Encyclopedia of the Continental Congress*. Armenia, New York: Grey House Publishing, 2015.

Hamilton, Edward P. *Fort Ticonderoga: Key to a Continent*. Boston: Little, Brown & Company, 1964.

Isenberg, Nancy. *Fallen Founder: The Life of Aaron Burr*. New York: Penguin Group, 2007.

Kennedy, Roger G. *Burr, Hamilton, and Jefferson: A Study in Character*. New York: Oxford University Press, 1999.

Kiernan, Denise & Joseph D'Agnese. *Signing Their Lives Away: The Fame and Misfortune of the Men Who Signed the Declaration of Independence*. Philadelphia: Quirk Books, 2008.

———. *Signing Their Rights Away: The Fame and Misfortune of the Men Who Signed the United States Constitution*. Philadelphia: Quirk Books, 2011.

Klarman, Michael J. *The Framers' Coup: The Making of the United States Constitution*. New York: Oxford University Press, 2016.

Langguth, A. J. *Patriots*. New York: Simon and Schuster, 1988.

Larson, Edward J. *A Magnificent Catastrophe*. New York: Free Press, 2007.

Lee, Mike. *Written Out of History: The Forgotten Founders Who Fought Big Government*. New York: Penguin Books, 2017.

Lewis, James E., Jr., *The Burr Conspiracy: Uncovering the Story of an Early American Crisis*, Princeton: Princeton University Press, 2017.

Lockridge, Ross Franklin. *The Harrisons*. 1941.

Lomask, Milton. *Aaron Burr: The Years from Princeton to Vice President, 1756-1805*. New York: Farrar Straus Giroux, 1979.

Lossing, Benson J. *Pictorial Field Book of the Revolution*. New York: Harper Brothers. 1851.

Maier, Pauline. *American Scripture: Making the Declaration of Independence*. New York: Alfred A. Knopf, Inc., 1997.

McCullough, David. *John Adams*. New York: Simon & Schuster, 2002.

Meltzer, Brad & Josh Mensch. *The First Conspiracy: The Secret Plot to Kill George Washington*. New York: Flat Iron Books. 2018.

Middlekauff, Robert. *The Glorious Cause: The American Revolution, 1763-1789*. Oxford: Oxford University Press, 2005.

Miller, Jr., Arthur P. & Marjorie L. Miller. *Pennsylvania Battlefields and Military Landmarks*. Mechanicsburg, Pennsylvania: Stackpole Books, 2000.

Millett, Allan R. & Peter Maslowski. *For the Common Defense: A Military History of the United States of America*. New York: The Free Press, 1984.

Moore, Charles. *The Family Life of George Washington*. New York: Houghton Mifflin, 1926.

Nagel, Paul C. *The Lees of Virginia: Seven Generations of an American Family*. Oxford: Oxford University Press, 1990.

O'Connell, Robert L. *Revolutionary: George Washington at War*. New York: Random House. 2019.

Racove, Jack N. *Revolutionaries: A New History of the Invention of America*. New York: Houghton Mifflin Harcourt, 2011.

Raphael, Ray. Founding Myths: *Stories That Hide Our Patriotic Past*. New York: MJF Books, 2004.

Rossiter, Clinton. *1787 The Grand Convention*. New York: The Macmillan Company, 1966.

Seymour, Joseph. *The Pennsylvania Associators, 1747-1777*. Yardley, Pennsylvania: Westholme Publishing, LLC. 2012.

Schweikart, Larry & Michael Allen. *A Patriot's History of the United States from Columbus's Great Discovery to the War on Terror*. New York: Penguin, 2004.

Sharp, Arthur G. *Not Your Father's Founders*. Avon, Massachusetts: Adams Media, 2012.

Stahr, Walter. *John Jay: Founding Father*. New York: Diversion Books, 2017.

Taafee, Stephen R. *The Philadelphia Campaign, 1777-1778*. Lawrence, Kansas: University of Kansas Press, 2003.

Tinkcom, Harry Marlin, *The Republicans and the Federalists in Pennsylvania, 1790-1801*. Harrisburg, Pennsylvania: Pennsylvania Historical and Museum Commission. 1950.

Ward, Matthew C. *Breaking the Backcountry: The Seven Years' War in Virginia and Pennsylvania, 1754-1765*. Pittsburgh, Pennsylvania: University of Pittsburgh Press, 2003.

Weisberger, Bernard A. *America Afire: Jefferson, Adams, and the Revolutionary Election of 1800*. New York: HarperCollins, 2000.

Wood, Gordon S. *The Radicalism of the American Revolution*. New York: Vintage Books, 1993.

———. *Empire of Liberty: A History of the Early Republic, 1789-1815*. New York: Penguin Books, 2004.

———. *Revolutionary Characters: What Made the Founders Different*. New York: Penguin Books, 2006.

————. *The Americanization of Benjamin Franklin*. Oxford: Oxford University Press, 2009.

Wright, Benjamin F. *The Federalist: The Famous Papers on the Principles of American Government: Alexander Hamilton, James Madison, John Jay*. New York: Metro Books, 2002.

Zobel, Hiller B. *The Boston Massacre*. New York: W. W. Norton & Company, 1970.

Video Resources:

Guelzo, Allen C. The Great Courses: *America's Founding Fathers* (Course N. 8525). Chantilly, Virginia: The Teaching Company, 2017.

Online Resources:

Archives.gov – for information on the Constitutional Convention.

CauseofLiberty.blogspot.com – for information on Daniel Carroll.

ColonialHall.com – for information about the signers of the Declaration of Independence.

DSDI1776.com – for information on many Founders.

FamousAmericans.net – for information on many Founders.

FindaGrave.com – for burial information, vital statistics and obituaries.

FirstLadies.org – for information on Abigail Adams.

Newspapers.com – Hundreds of newspaper articles were accessed—too numerous to mention here.

NPS.gov – for information on various park sites.

TeachingAmericanHistory.com – for information on Charles Pinckney and George Wythe.

TheHistoryJunkie.com – for information on multiple Founders.

USHistory.org – for information on multiple Founders.

Wikipedia.com – for general historical information.

Index

INDEX